First World War
and Army of Occupation
War Diary
France, Belgium and Germany

58 DIVISION
174 Infantry Brigade
London Regiment
2/7 Battalion
30 January 1915 - 27 February 1916

WO95/3005/7

Published by

The Naval & Military Press Ltd

Unit 10 Ridgewood Industrial Park,

Uckfield, East Sussex,

TN22 5QE England

Tel: +44 (0) 1825 749494

www.naval-military-press.com

www.nmarchive.com

This diary has been reprinted in facsimile from the original. Any imperfections are inevitably reproduced and the quality may fall short of modern type and cartographic standards.

© **Crown Copyright**
Images reproduced by permission of The National Archives, London, England, 2015.

Contents

Document type	Place/Title	Date From	Date To
Heading	WO95/3005/7		
Heading	2/7 London Regt. 1915 Aug-1916 Feb		
War Diary	Burgess Hill	30/01/1915	30/01/1915
War Diary	Burgess Hill	01/02/1915	31/03/1915
War Diary	Ipswich	31/03/1916	31/03/1916
War Diary	Burgess Hill	09/04/1915	19/04/1915
War Diary	Crowborough	30/04/1915	18/05/1915
War Diary	Norwich	18/05/1915	21/06/1915
War Diary	Ipswich	02/07/1916	23/08/1916
Miscellaneous	Statement 31st August 1915	31/08/1915	31/08/1915
War Diary	Ipswich	01/09/1915	02/11/1915
War Diary	Debenham	03/11/1915	03/11/1915
War Diary	Laxfield	04/11/1915	04/11/1915
War Diary	Halesworth	05/11/1915	05/11/1915
War Diary	Marlesford	06/11/1915	06/11/1915
War Diary	Ipswich	07/11/1915	27/02/1916

WO 95/3005/7

2/7 London Regt

1915 Aug — 1916 Feb

Army Form C. 2118.

WAR DIARY
or
INTELLIGENCE SUMMARY.
(*Erase heading not required.*)

Hour, Date, Place	Summary of Events and Information	Remarks and references to Appendices
Week ending Jan 30 1915 Burgen H.U.	Nothing to Report 4/4	

Army Form C. 2118.

WAR DIARY
or
INTELLIGENCE SUMMARY.
(Erase heading not required.)

Instructions regarding War Diaries and Intelligence Summaries are contained in F.S. Regs., Part II and the Staff Manual respectively. Title pages will be prepared in manuscript.

Hour, Date, Place	Summary of Events and Information	Remarks and references to Appendices
16.1.1915 BURGESS HILL 2nd 2-5th Sussex	12.45am. A biplane was seen by the B". from NORTH corner flying N.W. No marks could be observed and it was not considerable. Twice a between the observers and the sun. AH 4.15p. 3 biplanes flying Northwards reported to me by the Orderly Room Serjeant. They were all marked O.O. AH Nothing to Report	

2/7th Bn The London Regt

WAR DIARY
or
INTELLIGENCE SUMMARY.

Army Form C/2118.

3

(Erase heading not required.)

Hour, Date, Place	Summary of Events and Information	Remarks and references to Appendices
BURGESS HILL Week ending midnight Feb 14/15 1915 Feb 12	Nothing to Report. JHS At 1.7 pm. an aeroplane was seen from the Downs near [WINDMILLS] just East of CLAYTON TUNNEL The biplane was marked O.O. and was flying low and approximately Southward. JHS Aeroplane (approaching)	

Army Form C. 2118.

WAR DIARY
or
INTELLIGENCE SUMMARY.
(Erase heading not required.)

Instructions regarding War Diaries and Intelligence Summaries are contained in F. S. Regs., Part II. and the Staff Manual respectively. Title pages will be prepared in manuscript.

Hour, Date, Place	Summary of Events and Information	Remarks and references to Appendices

2/7th Bn The London Regt

WAR DIARY
or
INTELLIGENCE SUMMARY.
(Erase heading not required.)

Army Form C. 2118.

Hour, Date, Place	Summary of Events and Information	Remarks and references to Appendices
Feb 21. 1915 2.7 pm BURGESS HILL	Airship (apparently PARSEVAL type) seen from ROYAL OAK (Ord map 1" Sheet 39 Square E9) flying approximately ESE. The Red Ensign & White Ensign were streaming aft. It was flying at approximately 2000 feet. HW	
Feb 25th 1915 2.15pm	An airship (apparently the same one as above) was seen flying close to WIVELSFIELD flying W.N.W. HW	
Week ending midnight 26/27 Feb	Nothing else to Report H W Eden (Capt. Actg. Adjt)	

Army Form C. 2118.

WAR DIARY
or
INTELLIGENCE SUMMARY.
(Erase heading not required.)

Instructions regarding War Diaries and Intelligence Summaries are contained in F. S. Regs., Part II. and the Staff Manual respectively. Title pages will be prepared in manuscript.

Hour, Date, Place	Summary of Events and Information	Remarks and references to Appendices
BURGESS HILL		
Week ending midnight 5th March 1915	Nothing to Report	

A.H. Yee
Capt + Adj (a.b.)
2/17th the London Reg.

(73989) W4141—463. 400,000. 9/14. H.&J.Ltd. Forms/C. 2118/10.

Army Form C. 2118.

WAR DIARY
INTELLIGENCE SUMMARY.
(*Erase heading not required.*)

Instructions regarding War Diaries and Intelligence Summaries are contained in F. S. Regs., Part II. and the Staff Manual respectively. Title pages will be prepared in manuscript.

Hour, Date, Place	Summary of Events and Information	Remarks and references to Appendices
BURGESS HILL 3.10 P.M. March 9th.	British airship sighted over BURGESS HILL flying slowly in a N.E. direction.	

Army Form C. 2118.

8

WAR DIARY
or
INTELLIGENCE SUMMARY.
(Erase heading not required.)

Instructions regarding War Diaries and Intelligence Summaries are contained in F.S. Regs., Part II and the Staff Manual respectively. Title pages will be prepared in manuscript.

Hour, Date, Place	Summary of Events and Information	Remarks and references to Appendices
BURGESS+La Wool to midnight 1st–2nd March 1915	Nothing to Report. A.Speck Capt. Acting 2/7 KSLI the 1st day R.2.	

Army Form C. 2118.

WAR DIARY
INTELLIGENCE SUMMARY.

(Erase heading not required.)

Hour, Date, Place	Summary of Events and Information	Remarks and references to Appendices
Burgoo Hill		
20th March 1.10pm	Information as to 12 German Aeroplanes received from Bde Headquarters	
21st March 12.10pm	Telephone message from Brigade HQ - as to Zeppelin proceeding seawards (reported from CALAIS)	
	Nothing else to Report	

Edwin N. Dudley

Army Form C. 2118.

10

WAR DIARY
or
INTELLIGENCE SUMMARY.
(Erase heading not required.)

Place	Date	Hour	Summary of Events and Information	Remarks and references to Appendices
BURGESS HILL	March 30	3.55 pm	British Aeroplane travelling S.S.E. Seen from Orderly Room. AG	
	31	11.56 am	B.Plane travelling S.W. Seen from Orderly Room. AG	

M H Green
Capt & Act. Adjt
2/4 FB - The London Regt

Army Form C. 2118.

WAR DIARY
or
INTELLIGENCE SUMMARY. 2/7th B The London Regt
(Erase heading not required.)

Place	Date	Hour	Summary of Events and Information	Remarks and references to Appendices
IPSHUM	31/3/16		Nothing to Report for the month of March.	

R J Green
Captain O.C.
2/7th B The London Regt

Army Form C. 2118.

WAR DIARY
or
INTELLIGENCE SUMMARY.

(Erase heading not required.)

Place	Date	Hour	Summary of Events and Information	Remarks and references to Appendices
BURGESS HILL	Week ending Friday 9 April		Nothing to Report	
			Alfred	

WAR DIARY
INTELLIGENCE SUMMARY.

Army Form C. 2118.

12

Place	Date	Hour	Summary of Events and Information	Remarks and references to Appendices
BURKS HILL	April 18th	2.50 pm	Sergeant of the Civil Police reported a bomb explosion at SITTINGBOURNE. Reported. *Signature* Capt Adj	

Army Form C. 2118.

13

WAR DIARY
— or —
INTELLIGENCE SUMMARY.
(Erase heading not required.)

Place	Date	Hour	Summary of Events and Information	Remarks and references to Appendices
BURGESS HILL	April 14	8.30 am	"B" left for CROWBOROUGH in charge of Station Airships	
		2.53 pm	While on the march an Aeroplane (apparently of E.T.A. type) was seen to second A in FAIRWARP (in map sheet 39 from road just S of the SW corner of Square DII). The airship was flying very low and in an Easterly direction	

A. Green
Capt. ADS
for OC 217 HB- The Lovate Regt

Army Form C. 2118.

WAR DIARY
INTELLIGENCE SUMMARY.
(Erase heading not required.)

Hour, Date, Place	Summary of Events and Information	Remarks and references to Appendices
CROWBOROUGH Week ending mid-day 30. 4. 15	Nothing to Report AJGreen Capt + Adjt 2/7th B' The London Regt	

Army Form C. 2118.

15

WAR DIARY
INTELLIGENCE SUMMARY.
(Erase heading not required.)

Hour, Date, Place	Summary of Events and Information	Remarks and references to Appendices
CROWBOROUGH To May 7 1915	Nothing to Report MAgnew Capt & Adj 27th Bn The London Regt	

WAR DIARY
or
INTELLIGENCE SUMMARY.

Army Form C. 2118.

Place	Date	Hour	Summary of Events and Information	Remarks and references to Appendices
Crowborough Camp	14/4/15 Wednesday midnight		Nothing to Report	

R. Glynn
Capt + Adjt
3/4/15 3rd London Regt

Army Form C. 2118.

17

WAR DIARY
— or —
INTELLIGENCE SUMMARY.
(Erase heading not required.)

Instructions regarding War Diaries and Intelligence Summaries are contained in F.S. Regs., Part II. and the Staff Manual respectively. Title pages will be prepared in manuscript.

Hour, Date, Place	Summary of Events and Information	Remarks and references to Appendices
CROWBOROUGH May 18.	Bⁿ left CROWBOROUGH for NORWICH on change of stations. AH.	
NORWICH	Nothing to Report. AH	

AH Green
Capt. A/Adjt
2/7th Bⁿ The London Regt

Army Form C. 2118.

WAR DIARY
INTELLIGENCE SUMMARY.
(Erase heading not required.)

Hour, Date, Place	Summary of Events and Information	Remarks and references to Appendices
NORWICH Week to noon 28/5/15	Nothing to Report Allfrew Capt (a) 2/7KRB The London Regt	

Instructions regarding War Diaries and Intelligence Summaries are contained in F. S. Regs., Part II. and the Staff Manual respectively. Title pages will be prepared in manuscript.

WAR DIARY
or
INTELLIGENCE SUMMARY.
(*Erase heading not required.*)

Army Form C. 2118.

19

Hour, Date, Place	Summary of Events and Information	Remarks and references to Appendices
NORWICH June 1. 3pm	Aeroplane was seen by Major [illegible] flying W. It was flying very high and no details could be observed HLG	
	H L Green Capt + Adjt 2/7th Bn The London Regt 4/6/15	

(73989) W4141—463. 400,000. 9/14. H.&J.Ltd. Forms/C. 2118/10.

WAR DIARY
or
INTELLIGENCE SUMMARY.
(Erase heading not required.)

Army Form C. 2118.

20

Place	Date	Hour	Summary of Events and Information	Remarks and references to Appendices
NORWICH	June 6	10.10pm	Message received from Bde HQ Chief Constable Ipswich reports hostile aircraft in vicinity of CROMER. AAA County Borough Police reports hostile aircraft over SHERINGHAM. Information received by 1st London Div 9 pm 2.1 Bde 9.20 pm —	

MKflower Capt RA
2nd i/c The Lowland Regt

Place	Date	Hour	Summary of Events and Information	Remarks and references to Appendices
NORWICH	June 13	12.10 am	The following message received from HQ 3 Lond Inf Bde 11.13 pm AAA from IPSWICH police informs us a message from LANDGUARD FORT FELIXSTOWE states that a ZEPPELIN raid is to be expected tonight 3 ZEPPELINS have been sighted off the East Coast direction not ascertained. Further information follows to received AAA ends. From 21st LD IPSWICH. The following order by Capt D'ARCY LITTLE 2nd L Brigade. Inform guard to keep a strong lookout all night, and guard stand to arms on from Chief Constable (Norwich 29) Rec HQ 1403 Norwich) receipt further orders. Nothing was seen by the guard during the night. MH	

MHyen Capt adj 2/7th B Lond Rgt

WAR DIARY
or
INTELLIGENCE SUMMARY.

(Erase heading not required.)

Army Form C. 2118.

22

Place	Date	Hour	Summary of Events and Information	Remarks and references to Appendices
NORWICH	June 19	9.20 am	Change of Station NORWICH — IPSWICH	
		11.10 am		
	21	12.03 pm	Aeroplane (apparently monoplane) was seen by the B[?] from WOOLVERSTONE PARK. It was at a great height and details could not be discerned. The general course followed was Easterly. JH The aeroplane was also seen by the guard who reported the same to the Field Officer of the week who was present at the time. JH	

W Hman Capt (?)
217th Bn Welsh Regt

Army Form C. 2118.

WAR DIARY
INTELLIGENCE SUMMARY.
(Erase heading not required.)

Instructions regarding War Diaries and Intelligence Summaries are contained in F.S. Regs., Part II. and the Staff Manual respectively. Title pages will be prepared in manuscript.

Place	Date	Hour	Summary of Events and Information	Remarks and references to Appendices
IPSWICH	Week to Monday 2 July		Nothing to Report. Alfred (Capt a/d) 2/7th B - The London Regt	

Army Form C. 2118.

WAR DIARY
INTELLIGENCE SUMMARY.
(Erase heading not required.)

Hour, Date, Place	Summary of Events and Information	Remarks and references to Appendices
IPSWICH Week to July 9.	Nothing to Report. A Green Capt. ? for O.C. 2/17th Bn The London	

(73989) W4141—463. 400,000. 9/14. H.&J.Ltd. Forms/C. 2118/10.

Army Form C. 2118.

WAR DIARY
or
INTELLIGENCE SUMMARY.
(Erase heading not required.)

Instructions regarding War Diaries and Intelligence Summaries are contained in F. S. Regs., Part II. and the Staff Manual respectively. Title pages will be prepared in manuscript.

Place	Date	Hour	Summary of Events and Information	Remarks and references to Appendices
IPSWICH			Nothing to Report	
			J. B. Rusk?	
			2nd Lt. + Act. Adjt.	

Army Form C. 2118.

WAR DIARY
INTELLIGENCE SUMMARY.
(Erase heading not required.)

Instructions regarding War Diaries and Intelligence Summaries are contained in F. S. Regs., Part II. and the Staff Manual respectively. Title pages will be prepared in manuscript.

Place	Date	Hour	Summary of Events and Information	Remarks and references to Appendices
Ipswich	23/1/15		Nothing to Report	

M Lyser Capt RA
for O.C. 2/7th Bn = London Regt

Army Form C. 2118.

WAR DIARY
INTELLIGENCE SUMMARY.
(Erase heading not required.)

Instructions regarding War Diaries and Intelligence Summaries are contained in F.S. Regs., Part II. and the Staff Manual respectively. Title pages will be prepared in manuscript.

27

Place	Date	Hour	Summary of Events and Information	Remarks and references to Appendices
Ipswich	July 29	8.58 am	Aeroplane seen by Capt GREEN and Capt GODSON from RUSHMERE ST ANDREWS — MARTLESHAM ROAD at a point due South of L — LITTLE BEALINGS. The aeroplane was flying East at a great height & no marks or denotations were distinguishable	

A. Green
Capt (A)
for O.C. 2/11th Bn The London Regt

Army Form C. 2118.

WAR DIARY
INTELLIGENCE SUMMARY.
(Erase heading not required.)

Place	Date	Hour	Summary of Events and Information	Remarks and references to Appendices
IPSWICH		Week to midnight 5/6 August 1915	Nothing to Report MMGreen Capt Adjt 2/7th Bt The London Regt	

Army Form C. 2118.

WAR DIARY
or
INTELLIGENCE SUMMARY.
(Erase heading not required.)

Place	Date	Hour	Summary of Events and Information	Remarks and references to Appendices
Ipswich	Aug 12	11.30 pm	MS received from BdeHQ that ZEPPELINS were dropping bombs at WOODBRIDGE. Nothing was seen. A.A. Allpree Capt for OC 2/7 KRRS The London Regt	

Army Form C. 2118.

WAR DIARY
INTELLIGENCE SUMMARY.
(Erase heading not required.)

Place	Date	Hour	Summary of Events and Information	Remarks and references to Appendices
IPSWICH	Aug 17	9.20 pm	Order received from Bde HQ that ZEPPELINS were expected.	
			C. Coy took up allotted position	
		11. pm ⎱ midnight ⎰	At about these times it was thought that ZEPPELINS were heard but nothing was seen	
	18th	1.50 am	Order to return to billets was received.	

AH Green Capt & OC
2/7th B. The London Regt

Army Form C. 2118.

31

WAR DIARY
or
INTELLIGENCE SUMMARY.
(Erase heading not required.)

Instructions regarding War Diaries and Intelligence Summaries are contained in F. S. Regs., Part II. and the Staff Manual respectively. Title pages will be prepared in manuscript.

Place	Date	Hour	Summary of Events and Information	Remarks and references to Appendices
IPSWICH	Aug 22	9.13 pm	Order received from Bn HQ to take up anti aircraft posns	
			B Coy took up post	
	23	1.26 am	Order to return to Bn HQ who received	
			Nothing unusual was seen or heard by B Coy	AH

K Green Capt 2/8

for O.C. 2/7th B⁺ⁿ The London Regt.

STATEMENT.
31st. August, 1915.

<u>Unit.</u> 2/7th. Battalion, The London Regiment.
<u>Brigade.</u> 174th. Infantry Brigade.
<u>Division.</u> 58th (London) Division.
<u>Mobilization Centre.</u> Headquarters of Unit, 24, Sun Street,
Finsbury Square, London. E.C.
<u>Temporary War Station.</u> Ipswich.

Mobilization.   During this month a further 20 men who joined the Battalion with the draft of 600 recruits from the 3rd. Line Depot on June 4th, have had to be struck off strength as follows:

<u>Medical Grounds.</u>

    (a) Sent to the Provisional Battalion as fit for Home Service only................ 16.

    (b) Discharged as unfit....................... 3.

<u>Mis-statement as to age.</u> .... 1.

There was also a case of desertion and one death, making the total wastage 22, which with the previous discharges reduced the net total of the Draft to 388 remaining.

On Sunday August 15th a Draft of 200 men was sent to the 1st.Line Unit in France. Some difficulty was experienced by the officer in charge on arrival at Southampton with regard to obtaining rations for this Draft. Only bread and cheese could be procured the first day.

During the month no further recruits arrived from the 3rd.Line Depot. The men attached from that unit have been absorbed.

Ten men have rejoined from the Provisional Battalion as being over 18½ years of age.

There are now serving with the Battalion 98 men under the age of 19 years.

The present strength of the Battalion is 915 including

(2)

officers and all ranks.

Organization for defence.
On 13th August a party of 108 N.C.O's and men resumed rifle practice on the range at Felixstowe, when for 3 days 16 targets were allotted for use and afterwards for 2 days 32 targets. These men fired through Parts 1 and 2, and those qualified through Part 3. During the month a miniature range was constructed in the garden at "Lonsdale" house. About 200 men have had practice in firing on this range. About 130 are being got in readiness to fire on the full sized range at the first opportunity. It will facilitate training if the whole 32 targets can be used by the Battalion at one time.

For the purpose of teaching elementary musketry and for firing on the range it is quite impossible to avoid having to change rifles from man to man very frequently, thus making it difficult to carry out Brigade instructions regarding fixing responsibility of individuals for condition of rifles and accessories.

Training.
Owing to recruit drills and the necessity for giving preliminary musketry instruction and miniature rifle shooting to prepare men for firing on the range the number of men available for Battalion training is still limited. Much useful work, however, has been done in trench digging. A large piece of private ground has been placed at disposal of the Battalion for this purpose, and two opposing lines of fire trenches constructed with communication and cover trenches. These have been occupied all night by Companies of the Battalion and useful instruction has been derived by this means. Other night operations have taken place on training areas.

Physical training has been practised daily as well as

bayonet fighting.

Discipline. There is very little fault to find with the discipline of the Battalion.

Administration. (a) <u>Medical Services.</u>

The last inspection held by the Medical Officer took place on the 30th.inst. He reported that the men, with few exceptions, are fit and in good condition, also the condition of the Battalion as a whole is remarkably good considering the drafts which have been sent away and the inferior class of recruit which has been received. The Medical Officer has still to do duty for two battalions. This is a great strain on his time, and considering the difficulties he works under his services are very useful, but I think it very advisable that a Medical Officer should be sent to this Battalion so that he could devote his whole time to its needs. As both the battalions under the care present M.O's are on duty whenever an air raid is anticipated I should like to point out that in case of casualties arising from hostile aircraft there will be a very great strain on medical services.

(b) <u>Supply Services.</u>

Rations were issued to the Battalion for the first time at Ipswich on the 21st.inst, when four Central Feeding places were opened. The quality of the meat and rations provided has given complete satisfaction.

As all cooking has to be done in the open air, covered shelters are a necessity. Shortly after commencing Central Feeding I communicated with the D.C.R.E. on the subject of obtaining these shelters. No reply was received by me to my letter and as the wet weather set in shortly after Central Feeding commenced there was no alternative except to have shelters put up immediately, and this has been done at three of these Centres. I hope that the

(4)

cost of this will be allowed against the public.

(c) <u>Transport Services</u>.

Pack Saddles, Horse Blankets, Line Head Collars and Nose Bags are still urgently wanted. Nose Bags were indented for a very considerable time ago. Owing to their non-arrival there is a considerable wastage of forage, as the horses at present have to be fed on the bare ground. The oats supplied are poor in quality, and not up to 38 lbs per bushel.

The Battalion has now in its possession a Travelling Kitchen. It is proposed to use this in connection with Company Training so that all the cooks may obtain practice in connection with it.

(d) <u>Ordnance</u>.

The Battalion is still in want of Machine Guns. The tables in use at some of the Central Feeding Halls have been borrowed and are quite unsuited for the purpose of taking meals. D.A.D.O.S. has been requested to supply Regulation tables as soon as possible so that the men may be made more comfortable.

The Sand Bags issued to the Battalion are of very inferior quality. A number of them have burst as soon as filled with sand and lifted from the ground.

(e) <u>Clothing and Equipment</u>.

Since my last statement covers for water bottles have been received. The sets of equipment to replace those sent to the 100th. Provisional Battalion have been unpacked and issued.

(f) <u>Billeting</u>.

All ranks are now billeted as near as possible to their respective Company Feeding Centres. There is plenty of room in the district allotted to the Battalion.

Charles W. Berkeley.

Ipswich.
31/8/15.

Lieut. Col.
Commanding 2/7th. Battn.
The London Regt.

WAR DIARY
or
INTELLIGENCE SUMMARY.

(Erase heading not required.)

Army Form C. 2118.

Place	Date	Hour	Summary of Events and Information	Remarks and references to Appendices
IPSWICH	Sept 1	10.30 am	Practice entraining in emergency train	
	2		Training contd	
	3		Training Contd	
	3		Training Contd	
			Regimental Tour to Coy Commanders 2/Lt in Command under Major Horsfall	
			2/Lt STRINGER joined for duty	
	4		Training Con.d	
	5		Church Parade	
	6		Training contd – Musketry at FELIXSTOWE	
			Combined Staff Ride 2 of Artillery – 5 officers attended	
			2Lt SYMONDSON joined in his Company	
	7		Training contd	
			Regtl Tour to Coy Commanders + Coy 2nd in Command contd	

Army Form C. 2118.

WAR DIARY
or
INTELLIGENCE SUMMARY.
(Erase heading not required.)

Instructions regarding War Diaries and Intelligence Summaries are contained in F.S. Regs., Part II. and the Staff Manual respectively. Title pages will be prepared in manuscript.

Place	Date	Hour	Summary of Events and Information	Remarks and references to Appendices
IPSWICH	Sept 8		Training contd.	
	9	9.30 pm	Anti Zeppelin posⁿ taken up by C. Coy. Nothing unusual was seen or heard. MH	
		1.30 am	Training contd. MH	
	10th	9.2 pm	Anti ZEPPELIN posⁿ taken up by C. Coy. Nothing unusual was seen or heard. MH	
		1.30 am		
	11th		Training contd. MH	
		10.23 pm	Training contd. Anti Zeppelin posⁿ taken up by A. Coy. No Zeppelins were seen or heard. Some lights (apparently signalling) were seen. MH	
	12th	2.13 am		

1577 Wt.W10791/1773 500,000 1/15 D.D.&L. A.D.S.S./Forms/C/2118.

WAR DIARY
or
INTELLIGENCE SUMMARY.

(Erase heading not required.)

Army Form C. 2118.

Place	Date	Hour	Summary of Events and Information	Remarks and references to Appendices
IPSWICH	Sept 12 (Sun)		Church Parade.	
	12	11.45pm	Several reports were heard from a W. direction and sound as of aircraft passing Eastward over the town were heard.	
	13	1.0 am	Three loud reports were heard from the East. AH	
	14th		Training cont'd AH	
			Training cont'd.	
		10pm	Sounds as of aircraft passing W to E were heard. Bright flashes in the N were seen. AH	
	15th		Training cont'd AH	
	16th	6.50 pm	Piquet sent to BOURNE BRIDGE. Nothing unusual reported AH	
		12.30 am	No Motor Cars passed the Piquet	

Army Form C. 2118.

WAR DIARY
or
INTELLIGENCE SUMMARY
(Erase heading not required.)

Instructions regarding War Diaries and Intelligence Summaries are contained in F.S. Regs., Part II. and the Staff Manual respectively. Title pages will be prepared in manuscript.

Place	Date	Hour	Summary of Events and Information	Remarks and references to Appendices
IPSWICH	Sep 16		Training Contd. MH	
	17		Training cont'd MH	
	18		Training continued	
		6.25 pm	Message received from Bde. H.Q. at 6-25 p.m. "Papers for Tactical Exercise MH"	
			In other words Period of Vigilance Modified. P.R.?	
	19	a.m.		
		4.30	Message received from Bde. H.Q. to entrain in pursuance of scheme.	
		7-0 am	Battalion entrained	
		10.55	Battalion took up position at Pokehill Farm near Halesworth.	
		1-0 pm	Orders received from Bde. H.Q. to proceed back to Halesworth.	
		3-5 pm	Battalion detrained at Ipswich.	
		3.40 pm	Message received from Bde. H.Q. "Period of Vigilance now ended." LBA	
	20		Training continued. LBA	

Army Form C. 2118.

WAR DIARY
or
INTELLIGENCE SUMMARY.
(Erase heading not required.)

Instructions regarding War Diaries and Intelligence Summaries are contained in F. S. Regs., Part II. and the Staff Manual respectively. Title pages will be prepared in manuscript.

Place	Date	Hour	Summary of Events and Information	Remarks and references to Appendices
IPSWICH	Sept 21		Training contd. WK	
	22		Training contd. WK	
	23		Training contd. WK	
	24		Training contd. WK	
	25		Training contd WK	
	26		Church Parade WK	
	27		Training contd WK	
	28		Training contd WK	
	29		Training contd WK	
	30		Training contd WK	

Charles W. Roberty
Lieut.
O.C. 2/1 v. Butts. London Regt.

Army Form C. 2118.

3v

WAR DIARY
or
INTELLIGENCE SUMMARY.
(Erase heading not required.)

Place	Date	Hour	Summary of Events and Information	Remarks and references to Appendices
Ipswich	Week to Sept 4. 1915		Nothing to Report Allgreen Capt (?) for O.C. 2/7th B- The London Regt	

WAR DIARY
or
INTELLIGENCE SUMMARY.
(Erase heading not required.)

Army Form C. 2118.

33

Place	Date	Hour	Summary of Events and Information	Remarks and references to Appendices
IPSWICH	Sept 7	7.15 am	Aeroplane seen by guard. Flying N.E. Details not reported. Reported to Bde HQ. AH	
	8	8.0 pm	M.S. from 174th BDE. Phone up anti-ZEPPELIN posn. C Coy turn out to postn. AH	
	9	1.30 am	M.S. from 174th BDE to return to billets. Nothing unusual was seen or heard. No motor cars passed BOURNE BRIDGE AH	
	9	2 pm	M.S. from 174th BDE to phone up anti-ZEPPELIN posn - C Coy turn up posn	
	10th	1.25 am	M.S. received from 174th Bde to return to Billets at 1.30 am. 2 Motor Cars passed BOURNE BRIDGE AH Nothing unusual was seen or heard	

WAR DIARY
or
INTELLIGENCE SUMMARY.

Army Form C. 2118.

Instructions regarding War Diaries and Intelligence Summaries are contained in F.S. Regs., Part II. and the Staff Manual respectively. Title pages will be prepared in manuscript.

(Erase heading not required.)

Hour, Date, Place	Summary of Events and Information	Remarks and references to Appendices
Sept 11th 10.23 pm Orchard	Rifles fired against Aircraft. A Coy took up position.	
11 pm	No aircraft were seen or heard. (blue)	
1.30 am BRIDGE	Saw a rocket (red) fired due NORTH of BOURNE BRIDGE at 1.30 am.	The post at BOURNE
	During the whole time the picquet were on duty there were intermittent lights (apparently signalling) showing on the other (N.E.) bank of the river ORWELL.	
12th 2.13 am	Ms received from 17th R.H.M.P. One moss car passed BOURNE BRIDGE to go home. Ack.	
11.40 pm	Several shots were heard from the West and South afterwards. Sound as if coming from near the farm where No 5½ pickets were held. Reports taken.	
13th 1 am	Three loud reports were heard from the Entrance.	
	No orders these prisoners received Ack.	

WAR DIARY
INTELLIGENCE SUMMARY.
(Erase heading not required.)

Army Form C. 2118.

Place	Date	Hour	Summary of Events and Information	Remarks and references to Appendices
IPSWICH	Sep 1st	10pm	Attention being drawn to the location of shooting on the Railway, MAJOR MUSFORD, CAPT GREEN & CAPT SPEED went out and listened. The hum of aircraft was distinctly heard, and three bigger flashes (apparently from the ground) were seen. The Sound and flashes began in the West and moved gradually through North to Eastwards. Observation from the garden 217th Br. Officers Mess LONSDALE BEDSTEAD ROAD NH	
	Sep 15	8.50 pm	M/s from 174th Bde. to send out Piquet to BOURNE BRIDGE	
	16	2.30 am	Piquet withdrawn. Nothing unusual was seen or heard. No Motor Cars passed Piquet. NH	
		11.35 am	Aeroplane seen by CAPT GIBSON from Shippon Ground. Flying SW. NH	

Army Form C. 2118.

WAR DIARY
or
INTELLIGENCE SUMMARY.

(Erase heading not required.)

36

Place	Date	Hour	Summary of Events and Information	Remarks and references to Appendices
IPSWICH	Sept 17th	11 am	Biplane (details not distinguishable) was seen from MARTLESHAM HEATH, by Lt Col BERKELEY & other officers. It could round two or three times then approach Hn Nawards. It was flying low & at a considerable distance from the observer. ALh	
	18th	6.10 pm	Nil. JRT.	

WAR DIARY
INTELLIGENCE SUMMARY.

Army Form C. 2118.

Place	Date	Hour	Summary of Events and Information	Remarks and references to Appendices
Ipswich	Week ending Sept 25th		Nothing to Report	

H.J. New Capt w/s
2/7th Bn The London Regt

WAR DIARY
or
INTELLIGENCE SUMMARY.
(Erase heading not required.)

Army Form C. 2118.

52a [underlined 95
2/1 Oct/9/15 ?

Place	Date	Hour	Summary of Events and Information	Remarks and references to Appendices
PSWICH	Oct 2		Draft of 70 men (with 1 Officer & 1 Sgt as conducting party) arrived from 3rd Line Depot London. MLL	
	13	7.38 pm	Ms received from Bde HQ to turn out Anti Zeppelin parties. Aircraft were heard over BOURNE BRIDGE at 11.5 pm and 1.15 a.m. Nothing seen. No en passed [unclear]. Piquet returned at dawn. MLL	
	14th		Ms received from Bde Office that 3 officers were to be sent to the 11th Bn. Capt Jr WILSON 2Lt A MARTIN 2Lt PG BERRINGER [?]	
	14th		Ms received from Bde Office (B 390) stating that Capt WILSON should proceed first to effect two [unclear] further instructions MLL	

1577 Wt.W10791/1773 500,000 1/15 D.D. & L. A.D.S.S./Forms/C. 2118.

WAR DIARY
INTELLIGENCE SUMMARY

Army Form C. 2118.

Place	Date	Hour	Summary of Events and Information	Remarks and references to Appendices
PNICH	29 Oct		136 men proceeded to join 3rd Rine Depot 70th HLI	
	30 Oct		4 NCOS & 92 men proceeded to join 3rd Rine Depot 70th HLI	

Army Form C. 2118.

38

WAR DIARY
or
INTELLIGENCE SUMMARY.
(Erase heading not required.)

Instructions regarding War Diaries and Intelligence Summaries are contained in F. S. Regs., Part II. and the Staff Manual respectively. Title pages will be prepared in manuscript.

Place	Date	Hour	Summary of Events and Information	Remarks and references to Appendices
IPSWICH	2 Oct. 1915		Nothing to Report. Allgren Capt and 2/7 K.B. The London Regt	

Army Form C. 2118.

WAR DIARY
or
INTELLIGENCE SUMMARY.
(Erase heading not required.)

Instructions regarding War Diaries and Intelligence Summaries are contained in F. S. Regs., Part II. and the Staff Manual respectively. Title pages will be prepared in manuscript.

Place	Date	Hour	Summary of Events and Information	Remarks and references to Appendices
IPSWICH	5 Oct		(i) Nothing to Report (ILLICIT SIGNALLING)	
			(iii) AIRCRAFT Nothing unusual to report	
			(iv) MISCELLANEOUS INFORMATION Nil	

RWGreen
Capt Adj.
2/17th Bn The London Regt

Army Form C. 2118.

WAR DIARY
or
INTELLIGENCE SUMMARY.
(Erase heading not required.)

Place	Date	Hour	Summary of Events and Information	Remarks and references to Appendices
IPSWICH	Oct 13		1. — ILLICIT SIGNALLING NIL	
			11. AIRCRAFT	
		7.34 pm	Order received from BthHQ to take up Anti-Zeppelin posn	
		11.5 pm	} Sound of Zeppelins. Nothing was seen on either occasion	
	14th	1.5 am	Two cars passed BOURNE BRIDGE	
	11th		(2) NIL	

M. Green Capt (A/S)
2/7th Bn The London Regt

Army Form C. 2118.

WAR DIARY
or
INTELLIGENCE SUMMARY.
(Erase heading not required.)

Instructions regarding War Diaries and Intelligence Summaries are contained in F. S. Regs., Part II. and the Staff Manual respectively. Title pages will be prepared in manuscript.

41

Place	Date	Hour	Summary of Events and Information	Remarks and references to Appendices
IPSWICH	to 28/10/15		(1) ILLICIT SIGNALLING — NIL	
			(ii) AIRCRAFT — NIL	
			(iii) MISCELLANEOUS INFORMATION — NIL	
			H.H.Green	
			Capt. 2iC	
			2/7th B⁻ The London Regt	

1577 Wt.W10791/1773 500,000 1/15 D. D. & L. A.D.S.S./Forms/C. 2118.

WAR DIARY
or
INTELLIGENCE SUMMARY.

Army Form C. 2118.

42

Place	Date	Hour	Summary of Events and Information	Remarks and references to Appendices
Ipswich	28/8/15		ILLICIT SIGNALLING Nothing to Report	
			AIRCRAFT Nothing to Report	
			MISCELLANEOUS INFORMATION Nil	

Army Form C. 2118.

WAR DIARY
or
INTELLIGENCE SUMMARY.
(Erase heading not required.)

Instructions regarding War Diaries and Intelligence Summaries are contained in F. S. Regs., Part II. and the Staff Manual respectively. Title pages will be prepared in manuscript.

Place	Date	Hour	Summary of Events and Information	Remarks and references to Appendices
IPSWICH	2nd Nov	9.40 am	Detachment 2/7S (117 Officers & 450 Other Ranks) paraded for Brigade Trek	
DEBENHAM	3rd		Detachment billeted at DEBENHAM for night 2/3 Nov	
LAXFIELD	4th		(Head.Q. (Coy.) billeted at LAXFIELD } night 3/4 Nov 2 Coys at HORHAM	
HALESWORTH			Detachment billeted at HALESWORTH night 4/5 Nov	
MARLESFORD	6th		" " " MARLESFORD 5/6 "	
IPSWICH	7th		returned to IPSWICH.	

M Green
Capt (Adj)
2/7th S(uffolk)

Army Form C. 2118.

WAR DIARY
or
INTELLIGENCE SUMMARY.
(Erase heading not required.)

Nov. 15

Place	Date	Hour	Summary of Events and Information	Remarks and references to Appendices
IPSWICH	2nd Nov	8.40 am	Detachment of B'n (17 Officers 450 Other Ranks) paraded for Brigade Trek.	MH
DEBENHAM	3rd		Detachment billeted at DEBENHAM the night 2/3 Nov	MH
LAXFIELD	4th		(less 2 Coys) billeted at LAXFIELD } night 3/4 Nov 2 Coys at HORHAM	MH
HALESWORTH	5th		Detachment billeted at HALESWORTH night 4/5 Nov	MH
MARLESFORD	6th		" " " MARLESFORD 5/6 "	MH
IPSWICH	7th		" returned to IPSWICH.	MH

W. Mansford, Major
O.C. 2/7th Bn
The London Regt.

Alfred Capron
Captain
2/7th Bn The London Regt

WAR DIARY
INTELLIGENCE SUMMARY

Army Form C. 2118.

43

Place	Date	Hour	Summary of Events and Information	Remarks and references to Appendices
Ipswich	5/11/15	6 p.m.	On Tuesday, Nov. 2nd The 2/7th Battalion London Regiment, consisting of 17 Officers & 450 other ranks went on Brigade route which concludes tomorrow, 6th inst.	

Army Form C. 2118.

44

WAR DIARY
or
INTELLIGENCE SUMMARY.

(Erase heading not required.)

Instructions regarding War Diaries and Intelligence Summaries are contained in F.S. Regs., Part II. and the Staff Manual respectively. Title pages will be prepared in manuscript.

Place	Date	Hour	Summary of Events and Information	Remarks and references to Appendices
Ipswich	Nov 17		I ILLICIT SIGNALLING Nil	
			iii AIRCRAFT Nothing to Report	
			V MISCELLANEOUS INFORMATION Nil	

JH Green
Capt 1st
2/1 Herts Btn The London Regt

Army Form C. 2118.

WAR DIARY
or
INTELLIGENCE SUMMARY.
(Erase heading not required.)

45

Place	Date	Hour	Summary of Events and Information	Remarks and references to Appendices
Ipswich	Nov 19		i. ILLICIT SIGNALLING Nil. iii. AIRCRAFT Nothing to report v. MISCELLANEOUS INFORMATION. Nil. P. Holley-Jones 2/Lt Cmdr. 2/7th Bn The London Regt.	

1577 Wt. W10791/1773 50,000 1/15 D.D. & L. A.D.S.S./Forms/C. 2118

Army Form C. 2118.

WAR DIARY
INTELLIGENCE SUMMARY.
(Erase heading not required.)

Place	Date	Hour	Summary of Events and Information	Remarks and references to Appendices
IPSWICH	Nov 25 1915	—	i. ILLICIT SIGNALLING Nil. iii. AIRCRAFT Nil v. Miscellaneous Information Nil Alfred Capt. I.O. 2/17th KB" The London Regt	

WAR DIARY / INTELLIGENCE SUMMARY

Army Form C. 2118.

47

Place	Date	Hour	Summary of Events and Information	Remarks and references to Appendices
IPSWICH	Dec 3		1. ILLICIT SIGNALLING Nil 2. AIRCRAFT Nil 3. MISCELLANEOUS INFORMATION Nil [signed] Wyper (Capt. M.D.) 2/9 H.B. The London Regt	

Army Form C. 2118.

WAR DIARY
or
INTELLIGENCE SUMMARY.
(Erase heading not required.)

48

Place	Date	Hour	Summary of Events and Information	Remarks and references to Appendices
IPSWICH	10/5/15		i. ILLICIT SIGNALLING NIL ii. AIRCRAFT Nothing to Report v. MISCELLANEOUS INFORMATION NIL Allen Capt-D, for O.C. 2/7th 13th Middlesex Regt	

WAR DIARY
INTELLIGENCE SUMMARY

Army Form C. 2118.

Place	Date	Hour	Summary of Events and Information	Remarks and references to Appendices
IPSWICH	Dec 17th		(i) ILLICIT SIGNALLING see XX (ii) AIRCRAFT Nothing to Report XX (iii) MISCELLANEOUS INFORMATION see XX	

Alfred (Cognard)
2/7th Bn The London Regt

Army Form C. 2118.

WAR DIARY
or
INTELLIGENCE SUMMARY.
(Erase heading not required.)

Instructions regarding War Diaries and Intelligence Summaries are contained in F. S. Regs., Part II and the Staff Manual respectively. Title pages will be prepared in manuscript.

50

Place	Date	Hour	Summary of Events and Information	Remarks and references to Appendices
IPSWICH	Dec 4th 1915		i. ILLICIT SIGNALLING Nil ii. AIRCRAFT Nothing to Report iii. MISCELLANEOUS INFORMATION Nil M Glover (Capt ?) for O.C. 27th 18th Territorial Regt	

WAR DIARY or INTELLIGENCE SUMMARY

Army Form C. 2118.

Place	Date	Hour	Summary of Events and Information	Remarks and references to Appendices
IPSWICH	8/4/18		I. ILLICIT SIGNALLING Nil	
			II. AIRCRAFT Nothing to Report	
			III. MISCELLANEOUS INFORMATION Nil	

Wyler
Capt TC
2/7 K.B. Yorkshire Regt

Army Form C. 2118.

WAR DIARY
or
INTELLIGENCE SUMMARY.
(Erase heading not required.)

Instructions regarding War Diaries and Intelligence Summaries are contained in F. S. Regs., Part II. and the Staff Manual respectively. Title pages will be prepared in manuscript.

Place	Date	Hour	Summary of Events and Information	Remarks and references to Appendices
IPSWICH	31/12/15		Nothing to Report during month of December 1915	[Stamp: 58th (LONDON) DIVISION 2 - JAN.1916 GENERAL STAFF]

Charles W. Berkeley
Lt. Col.
Comdg 2/1 North'n Gz London Ryt.

WAR DIARY
or
INTELLIGENCE SUMMARY.

Army Form C. 2118.

Place	Date	Hour	Summary of Events and Information	Remarks and references to Appendices
IPSWICH			Nothing to Report during month of December 1915 2/7TH BATTALION, THE LONDON REGT. Edwin H. Bulkeley Lt Colonel Comdg 2/7 Bn. The London Regt	

Army Form C. 2118.

WAR DIARY
or
INTELLIGENCE SUMMARY.

(Erase heading not required.)

2/7th Bn The London Regt

Place	Date	Hour	Summary of Events and Information	Remarks and references to Appendices
IPSWICH	Jan 27		First Batch of John Resources arrived. WG	
	28		2/Lt PHALLEY JONES & 2/Lt SIMONS 10th Bn E Surr Regt attd were transferred. WG	
	28	9/50 pm	A.B. Corps turned out to take up anti-Zeppelin positions. Dismissed midnight. 26/Lyk WG	

[Stamp: 56th (LONDON) DIVISION 3 FEB 1916 GENERAL STAFF]

J.M. Green
Lt (Captain)
2/7th Bn The London Regt

WAR DIARY or INTELLIGENCE SUMMARY

Army Form C. 2118.

2/7th Bn The London Regt

(Erase heading not required.)

Place	Date	Hour	Summary of Events and Information	Remarks and references to Appendices
IPSWICH	Jan 21		First Batch of berlin Reservists arrived WH	
	28		2/Lt PHALLEY JONES & 2/Lt SIMONS 10th Bn E Surrey Regt attd were Transferred WH	
	2R	9.50 pm	A & B Coys turned out to take up anti-Zeppelin positions. Zeppelin midnight. Dismissed midnight. 2nd Regt WH	

W Green
(Captain)
2/7th Bn The London Regt

Army Form C. 2118.

WAR DIARY
or
INTELLIGENCE SUMMARY

2/17th B'n The London Regt

(Erase heading not required.)

Instructions regarding War Diaries and Intelligence Summaries are contained in F. S. Regs., Part II. and the Staff Manual respectively. Title pages will be prepared in manuscript.

Place	Date	Hour	Summary of Events and Information	Remarks and references to Appendices
IPSWICH	Jan 21		22 Reservists (Derby men) joined JW	
	22		16 " " " "	
	24		13 " " " "	
	25		29 " " " "	
	26		17 " " " "	
	27		6 " " " "	
	28		9 " " " "	
	29	9/50 pm	A & B Coys turned out to take up anti-Zeppelin positions. They were dismissed at midnight 28 Aug 16 JW	
	29		15 Reservists (Derby men) joined JW	
	31		11 " " JW	

W.J. Green (Capt A/L)
2/17th B'n The London Regt

Army Form C. 2118.

WAR DIARY
or
INTELLIGENCE SUMMARY
(Erase heading not required.)

Instructions regarding War Diaries and Intelligence Summaries are contained in F. S. Regs., Part II. and the Staff Manual respectively. Title pages will be prepared in manuscript.

Place	Date	Hour	Summary of Events and Information	Remarks and references to Appendices
Ipswich	Jan 21	2	22 Reservists Class B arrived ("Derby Men")	
	22		69 ditto	
	24		13 ditto	
	25		29	
	26		75	
	27		86 } ditto	
	28		9	
	29			
	31			

Army Form C. 2118.

WAR DIARY
or
INTELLIGENCE SUMMARY.
(Erase heading not required.)

Instructions regarding War Diaries and Intelligence Summaries are contained in F. S. Regs., Part II. and the Staff Manual respectively. Title pages will be prepared in manuscript.

Place	Date	Hour	Summary of Events and Information	Remarks and references to Appendices
Ipswich	Jan 21	2	Reservists Class B arrived (Selby Men)	
	22	16	ditto	
	24	13	ditto	
	25	29	} ditto	
	26	17		
	27	8		
	28	9		
	29	9		
	31			

WAR DIARY
or
INTELLIGENCE SUMMARY

Army Form C. 2118.

2/7th Bn Relievin Regt

Place	Date	Hour	Summary of Events and Information	Remarks and references to Appendices
PSNWR 7th	1		12" Anty Reshrnh 1 Offrs 7 M/h	
	2		2 " " "	
	3		21 " " "	
	4		4 " " "	
	9		12 " " "	
	10		6 " " "	
	11		14 M/h	
	12		21 M/h	
	13		2 Lieut M H Ireland + 2 Lieut A de Lemos transferred from 3/0 Lanc dep Rty	
	14		50 M/h Reservists 1 offrs 7 M/h	
	15		3 " " "	
	16		15 men 10 M/h Fin wef Proc B- M/h	
	20		2/Lieut H Brunson transferred from 3/rd Lanc Depot M/h M/greg (Copy in)	
	27			

WAR DIARY
or
INTELLIGENCE SUMMARY.

Army Form C. 2118.

2/7th B. The [...]

Place	Date	Hour	Summary of Events and Information	Remarks and references to Appendices
B witch	7th			
	1		12" Sub. Resolved 10 ms 7 MM	
	2		2 "	
	3		21 "	
	4		4 "	
	9		12 "	
	10		6 "	
	11		14 MM	
	12		21 MM	
	13		2 Lieut R.H. Ireland + 2 Lieut A. McLaren transferred from 3/7 Sept MM	
	14		50 Subs Reserve B 10 ms 7 MM	
	15,16		3 " - " MM	
	26		15 men 1st/7 Hr. 2nd/7 transferred from MM	
	27		2/Lieut H. Bealson transferred from 3rd/7 to 2nd/7th Myres (Mayo 7th)	